CW00538776

OREP
EDITIONS

Zone tertiaire de Nonant - 14400 BAYEUX
Tel: 02 31 51 81 31 - Fax: 02 31 51 81 32
info@orepeditions.com - www.orepeditions.com

Editor: Grégory Pique
Coordination editorial: Joëlle Meudic
Graphique design: OREP - Layout: Laurent Sand
English translation: Heather Inglis

ISBN: 978-2-8151-0412-8 - Copyright OREP 2018
Legal Deposit: 2nd quarter 2018

Cover: Soldiers from the 1st South Lancashire crossing what would later become Pegasus Bridge the day after landing on Sword Beach. © IWM

2   Aerial view of Bénouville bridge. We can clearly see Major Howard's three gliders, the German trenches and the east entrance to the bridge. © IWM

INTRODUCTION

'We landed in a terrible din. Suddenly, I could see nothing. I thought I was blind, but it was just my helmet over my eyes. As I straightened it, I saw that the glider had suffered damage and I also noticed a beam. We were just 47 yards from the bridge!

Our first problem was to capture the bunker next to the bridge for it housed the destruction system control button. It was capital. Our mission was to capture the bridge intact and to keep it so. We put the bunker out of action by throwing grenades and bombs with short fuses inside.

As we crossed the bridge, I heard a terrible noise behind me. Two other gliders had just landed. These soldiers were welcome. One group went to occupy the opposite side of the bridge; the other took up position in the German trenches next to the bunker. Parachuted troops arrived around half an hour after we did, before the Germans, who were in great numbers in the villages around this strategic point, had the time to react. They attacked fifteen minutes later. A tank arrived at the end of the road. We put it out of action. It burned for half an hour.'

John Howard, Commander of
the Ox and Bucks' Company D

'Holding the Line', the watchword of the Churchill 'bulldog'. Indeed, for a whole year, Britain was to hold the line, alone against the Axis. © NARA

CREATION OF THE BRITISH AIRBORNE ARMY

The victory of the German armies in France in May and June 1940 was an absolute catastrophe for the United Kingdom, both strategically and tactically. The country found itself alone against the Axis powers and although its Prime Minister Winston Churchill bravely declared in the Commons that the British would wage war by land, sea and air and that they would never surrender, no one believed in His Majesty's Kingdom's chances of holding back the Nazi surge. Tactically, the Germans had also surpassed the Allies in all fields, with the exception of the Navy. The invasion of *panzers* from the Ardennes to Manche had called all conceptions into question. Similarly, the use of airborne forces in the Netherlands or on the Meuse to capture vital defensive positions, such as Fort Eben-Emael, unveiled a new tactical spirit, at a time when the United Kingdom boasted no such force.

The capture of Fort Eben-Emael

This Belgian fort was the key element in the defensive line on the Albert Canal and the Meuse in 1940. On the 10th of May 1940, a unit of nine German gliders landed direct in the middle of the fort and the pioneers neutralised its cupolas using hollow charges. The Belgian garrison surrendered the following day.

A parachute unit aboard a Dakota during the Mush exercise on 22nd April 1944. © IWM

Churchill, as energetic as ever, could not accept this state of affairs and in July 1940, he exhorted the British high command to create an airborne force of 5,000 men as quickly as possible. Britain needed to catch up on its backwardness in the field, all the more so since Churchill had no intention of standing put, arms at the ready. With his country threatened with invasion, he planned to launch harassment operations along the Atlantic coast and parachutists were the ideal tool.

On the 24th of June, Major John Rock was entrusted with the challenging task of creating this force from scratch. With help from RAF Squadron Leader Strange, they set up an airborne troop training school at the Ringway airfield near Manchester, but they still had no men, no planes and no reliable parachute. Six obsolete Armstrong Whitworth Whitley planes were finally recovered and the first recruits began to arrive.

The X-Type parachute was also developed and adopted. Sparing no pains, Rock organised the very first jump on the 13th of July, just three weeks after his appointment. With the first unit formed, the N° 2 Commando became the 11th Special Air Service Brigade on the 21st of November 1940. The aim was not only to comprise an elite parachute force, but also to create a glider airborne unit.

A para from the same unit preparing to jump. The British only had one back parachute, whereas the Americans also wore an emergency chest parachute. However, the jumps in these operations lasted no more than 20 to 30 seconds,

The same unit as the previous picture, during the exercise on 22nd April 1944. The 3-day Mush exercise opposed the two British airborne divisions. The 6th Airborne played the German role. © IWM

The first jump within the framework of operation Colossus was made on the 7th of February 1941. N° 2 Commando's X Troop, commanded by Major Pritchard, was to destroy the Tragino aqueduct in Italy. The structure brought fresh water to the port of Taranto, an important base for the *Regia Marina*. The mission met with partial failure for, even if the British paras had achieved their objective, they were captured before being able to reach the submarine that was supposed to evacuate them and the aqueduct rapidly resumed its purpose.

For the rest of the year 1941, parachute forces continued to increase to finally reach sufficient numbers to form a brigade. Brigadier Frederick Browning was appointed commander of these forces in May.

A truly inspiring wife

Frederick Browning was married since 1932 to the famous novelist Daphne du Maurier, who wrote – among other works – Rebecca, a film adaptation of which was later produced by Alfred Hitchcock.

It is said that she was behind the choice of the insignia designed by Edward Seago, representing the winged horse Pegasus, ridden by Bellerophon, as the emblem of the British parachute forces. She is also said to have suggested to her husband to use the red and blue colours of his race horses on the paras' emblem. Finally, as from 1942, planes were equipped with a receiver which enabled the signal emitted by a beacon placed on the ground by reconnaissance scouts to be received in order to precisely located the jump zone. Hence, Browning baptised his receiver Rebecca.

The second raid led by the parachutists was successful. On the 27th of February, 119 paras commanded by Major Frost, seized elements of the German radar in Bruneval, near the Antifer headland to the north of Le Havre, before destroying it and being evacuated by sea.

At the end of the same year, the British airborne forces, now sufficient to form a division, engaged in combat in Tunisia. It was during these operations that the Germans nicknamed them the Red Devils, inspired by the colour of their berets. Then followed the operations in Sicily in 1943. Pathfinder units were deployed for the first time. These reconnaissance scouts were dropped before the major wave of troops in order to precisely mark out the dropping zones. However, operations met with a number of major setbacks. Strong winds scattered the parachutists and gliders, and many craft were the target of both enemy and friendly fire. For the operation to be launched in Normandy in June 1944, it was decided that large black and white

The royal family, George VI, his wife and their daughter, future Queen Elisabeth II, visiting units from the 6th Airborne Division on 19th May 1944 and passing in front of a 75mm howitzer. General Gale, the unit's commander, can be seen on the left. © IWM

On the 7th of December 1941, the 'Infamous Day' as Roosevelt proclaimed, several American ships were ablaze in Pearl Harbor, including the battleships *Tennessee* and *West Virginia*. © NARA

bands would be painted on the allied planes to distinguish them from the enemy.

Finally, the day before D-Day, General Browning was in command of two complete British airborne divisions, the 1st and the 6th. The parachutists had acquired four years' experience and training and were ready to support the large-scale landing operation that was planned in Normandy in June 1944.

ROLE OF THE 6TH AIRBORNE DIVISION IN OPERATION NEPTUNE

Even if the parachutists were in force and conducted sabotage missions, Churchill was well aware that he could not elaborate an amphibious operation capable of forcing the Germans out of the Continent alone. After a year of solitary combat against the Axis forces, the United Kingdom was finally joined in its struggle by the Soviet Union and the United States in 1941. The former put an end to the pact it had concluded with Hitler in 1939 after it was invaded. The United States had no choice but to join the conflict after the surprise attack on the Pearl Harbor naval base in Hawaii.

The British Prime Minister Winston Churchill and the American President Franklin D. Roosevelt at the Casablanca conference in 1943, during which they decided that the Axis Powers must surrender without conditions. © NARA

But no longer being alone was not enough. Churchill needed to elaborate a common strategy with the American President Franklin Roosevelt, if they wanted to crush the Axis. And that was going to be no picnic, far from it. The majority of the American chiefs were keen to concentrate their main efforts against Japan. Churchill finally managed to convince Roosevelt that Nazi Germany was the most urgent enemy to defeat. Such was the principle of the Germany First strategy devised in January 1942

BACK 'EM UP

BUY *EXTRA* BONDS

during the Arcadia conference. The Americans later placed priority on plans that directly targeted North-West Europe, whereas the British adopted a more pragmatic angle, preferring 'peripheral' operations aimed at dispersing the Axis forces whilst weakening them. It was within the context of this strategy that the first amphibious operations were launched in North Africa in November 1942 and in Italy in 1943.

The idea of a direct attack on the northwest of the European continent had not for as much been abandoned. A series of conferences in 1943 resulted in an outline plan. In Washington, in May, it was decided that the Landings would take place a year later, on the 1st of May 1944. Then in Quebec, in October, the landing zone was chosen: it would be Normandy which, although a greater distance from the British shores, offered the immense advantage of being less fortified than northern France. Finally, in December, the three leaders, Churchill, Roosevelt and Stalin discussed the opening of a 'Second Front' during the Eureka conference in Tehran.

The SHAEF. From left to right: General Bradley, Commander of the US First Army, Admiral Ramsay, Naval Force Commander, Air Marshal Tedder, Second in Command, General Eisenhower, Supreme Commander, General Montgomery, Commander of ground forces, Air Commander Leigh Mallory and General Bedell-Smith, Chief of Staff.
@ Mémorial de Caen

Since April 1943, the inter-Allied staff, the COSSAC (Chief of Staff to the Supreme Allied Commander), placed under General Morgan's command, had been working on the plans of this unprecedented amphibious operation. In December, General Eisenhower was appointed chief of the SHAEF (Supreme Headquarters Allied Expeditionary Force) taking over from Morgan. Very quickly, and in concertation with General Montgomery, commander of land forces, he grasped that the plan devised by the COSSAC lacked the power required to succeed the landing operation. Rather than the three and a half divisions initially to be engaged in the first assault (operation Neptune), they decided to engage six divisions with support from three airborne divisions. Furthermore, the landing zone was extended to now stretch from the base of the Cotentin peninsula to the Orne estuary.

On the 17th of February, General Browning, chief of the British airborne forces, informed General Gale of the mission that was to be entrusted to his 6th Airborne Division. Created in April 1943, this unit was to be dropped between the Orne and the Dives,

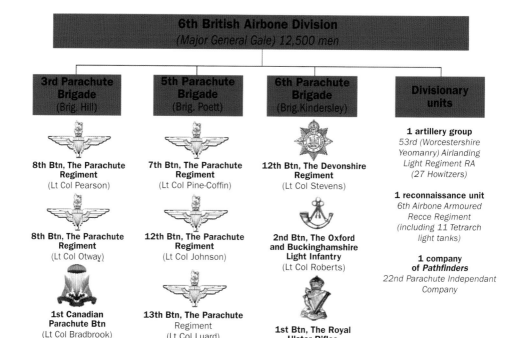

Major General Richard Nelson Gale

Born in 1896 in Wandsworth on the outskirts of London, Richard Gale entered the Royal Military Academy Sandhurst in 1915, in the midst of the Great War during which he was awarded the Military Cross. He spent the post-war years in India to return to England in 1936. He engaged in World War II with the rank of Major. The 1st Parachute Brigade was created in September 1941. General Alan Brooke, commander of the home forces, was positively impressed by Gale's leadership qualities and he entrusted him with the command of the brigade. In May 1943, he was placed in command of the 6th Airborne Division and was to plan the division's various missions for the Landings. After three months of combat in Normandy, Gale and his division returned to England. In December, he became second-in-command to General Brereton, in the First Allied Airborne Army before being appointed commander of the British 1st Airborne Corps. He was sent to India to fight against the Japanese, but the war came to an end before his unit engaged in combat. After the war, he took on several positions in Egypt then in Europe, where, in 1958, he replaced General Montgomery as Deputy Supreme Allied Commander. He retired in 1960 and died in 1982.

Major General Richard Nelson Gale. © IWM

to the east of the landing zone. Hence, it would cover the British amphibious operation on Sword Beach, on the opposite bank of the Orne. Two bridges across the river and its canal were to be captured intact in order to make the link with the troops landed on Sword. On the contrary, five bridges over the Dives and the Divettes were to be destroyed to prevent the arrival of German reinforcements from the north of France. Finally, the coastal artillery battery in Merville, equipped with 150mm guns and a possible threat to the landings on Sword Beach, needed to be neutralised. The drop would take place by night, over three phases. The parachutists from the 3rd and 5th Brigades would be the first to jump as from 0.50am, then Gale's HQ would follow with heavy equipment brought in by glider at 3.20am (operation Tonga). Finally, at 9pm, the 6th Airborne Brigade would land to the west of the Orne (operation Mallard).

A number of constraints complicated this mission. First of all, the drop was to be made by night, hence the necessity to use Pathfinders to mark out the Dropping Zones: a task that was entrusted to 60 men who would position the Eureka beacons that would emit the signal received by the lead planes in the formation transporting the parachutists. These scouts were also equipped with holophane lamps which they were to lay out to form a T.

Lieutenant Midwood giving the last instructions to his Pathfinders who are to mark out Dropping Zone K to the west of Touffréville. © IWM

These men are loading a six-pound antitank gun onto a Horsa glider. The parachute units often benefited from an element of surprise but needed to be rapidly reinforced by heavy weapons to counter enemy armoured attacks. © IWM

A further hurdle: to capture the bridges over the Orne and its canal, in Bénouville and Ranville, intact. The operation would need to be rapidly executed by a sufficiently strong unit to prevent the German garrisons from destroying them. Deploying parachutists for the task would inevitably result in troop dispersal and too long a delay to rejoin forces and attack. Finally, it was decided that gliders would be used to bring men in relatively silently, whilst maintaining unit cohesion. After selection exercises, Major John Howard's 2nd Battalion's Company D, the Oxford and Buckinghamshire Light Infantry, aka the Ox and Bucks, was selected in April 1944. Howard then set to training his unit to ensure the success of this surprise attack. He divided his company into six groups of 30 airborne soldiers and sappers. Each group was trained to accomplish its specific mission. A month prior to the Landings, Howard organised a six-day exercise in Countess Wear, where there were two bridges similar to those in Bénouville and Ranville. To make the exercise even more realistic, the defenders were dressed in German uniforms. Late May, each man was more than ready to fulfil this extremely perilous mission.

The Horsa glider

The use of gliders for military operations had been initiated by the Germans in Belgium during the capture of Fort Eben-Emael. The British were quick to grasp the usefulness of this type of craft which enables an entire unit to be positioned behind the enemy lines without troop dispersal. The very first Horsa gliders were delivered to the British Army in May 1942. This glider made of counterveneer had a wingspan of around 90 feet and could transport 30 men or heavy material (jeep, gun, etc.). The Hamilcar, another glider model, was even capable of transporting a Tetrarch light tank or a bulldozer.

© IWM

In April 1944, Brig. Hill informed Lt. Colonel Otway, chief of the 9th Parachute Battalion, that his unit had been chosen to neutralise the Merville artillery battery. Just like Howard, Otway had a number of photographs at his disposal to elaborate his

The parachutists were given some French money before heading for Normandy. © IWM

plan of attack. A life-size replica of the battery was even built near Newbury. His 750 paras eventually knew the site by heart, each one perfectly familiar with his mission. Three gliders were even to land directly inside the fortified position to complete the neutralisation operation.

By late May, all the men engaged in the 6th Airborne Division were positioned in secured camps. They were only to leave them when the time came to head for the airfield, take off and accomplish the mission they had taken several months to prepare.

A share of the 6th Airborne Brigade patiently waiting at the Tarrant Rushton airfield on the 6th of June. In the evening, it would reinforce the parachutists dropped between the Orne and the Dives by bringing in heavy material (guns, jeeps and even bulldozers). © IWM

THE *21. PANZER* AMBUSHED

As from 1942, it became evident to the Germans that the Allies would land at some point in time, most probably in northern France, where the distance from England is the shortest. Hitler then ordered for the construction of a whole series of fortifications, from Norway to the Spanish border, to prevent any invasion. Along the shoreline, strongpoints were established around antitank guns which were often housed in casemates. These *Wiederstandnesten* were surmounted with machine guns, flamethrowers, mortars and barbed wire. They were intended to stop the waves of assault from the sea, by inflicting deadly gunfire. Further inland, large calibre guns were grouped together to form artillery batteries, designed to destroy any allied ships offshore.

In December 1943, Hitler appointed *Generalfeldmarschall* Erwin Rommel as inspector of these coastal defences, referred to in German propaganda as the 'Atlantic Wall'. Rommel was quick to grasp that much work remained to be done if he wanted to increase the chances of effectively driving back the Allies. In the Nord region, the most exposed sector, the various fortified constructions were well underway and several divisions already in position to the rear. However, in Normandy, several batteries remained incomplete and the coast was only defended by a line of defensive forces without sufficient depth. He set to reinforcing the entire defensive system he was in charge of. He multiplied inspections to galvanise his troops and to accelerate construction work. He obtained supplementary units, in Normandy in particular, in order to reduce the sector to be covered by each division. Hence, the *352. Infanterie.Division* took charge of coastal defences in western Calvados, which enabled the *716. Infanterie Division* to reduce by half the zone it was to defend in the Bessin area and to the north of Caen.

Rommel also devised a whole series of obstacles to be installed direct on the beaches. These concrete tetrahedrons, chevaux de frise and mined stakes installed along the foreshore were designed to tear open the landing barges as they arrived by high tide. And if, on the contrary, the Allies should

A unit from the 716. Infanterie Division during one of the exercises that were part of the daily lives of the German soldiers prior to the Landings.
© Bundesarchiv

Field Marshal Rommel, with his staff, inspecting progression of the installation of beach obstacles upon his initiative. At high tide, they were to be totally submerged and to prevent the landing barges from approaching. © *Bundesarchiv*

decide to avoid these obstacles by landing at low tide, the defenders could easily reach their targets for they would have to cross a far longer stretch of beach. Rommel also undertook to have stakes placed in fields to prevent gliders from making a trouble-free landing. These stakes were soon to be baptised Rommel's asparagus.

Within this defensive system, the German marshal knew from experience that the *Panzerdivisionen* would play a vital role. He hoped to place them as close as possible to the beaches, in order to counter-attack allied troops before they could establish solid positions. However, *Generalfeldmarschall* von Runstedt preferred to keep these armoured divisions at a distance from the beaches and to group them together in a powerful *Panzergruppe* to forcefully counter-attack the Allies. This *Panzerkontroverse* was but partly solved by Hitler himself, who decided to meet halfway. Of the six *Panzerdivisionen* positioned to the north of the River Loire, he decided to allocate three to Rommel and kept control of the other three. Hence, the *21. Panzer*-Division reached the sector to the south of Caen in March 1944.

Men from the *21. Panzer Division* during inspection. In this case, a free-standing artillery piece on a spoiled French Hotchkiss chassis. © *Bundesarchiv*

© Rights reserved

This division, veterans of the Africa campaign, had been destroyed in Tunisia. It was reformed in July 1943 in the region around Rennes and was equipped, in particular, with spoiled French tanks which were restored and mounted with German artillery pieces. In June 1944, the division comprised two *Panzergrenadier* regiments, the 125th and the 192nd, and of one *Panzer*, the 22nd, i.e. a total of 218 tanks and 17,000 men.

Under the orders of *Generalleutnant* Feuchtinger, this unit was a genuine threat, not only to the forces that were to land on Sword Beach, but also for the troops from the 6th Airborne Division, who had no substantial antitank equipment. Major Hans von Luck's *Panzer Grenadier Regiment 125*, the headquarters of which were established in Vimont, less than 12 miles from Ranville, was capable of rapidly counter-attacking Gale's paras. Yet, when the first units jumped between the Orne and the Dives, Feuchtinger was not at his command post in Saint-Pierre-sur-Dives, but in the arms of his mistress in Paris, impossible to contact for several hours. A welcome delay for the Allies.

Field Marshal Rommel and General Feuchtinger in conversation in May 1944. Neither of them would be in Normandy on the 6th of June. © *Bundesarchiv*

GO TO IT

Early June 1944, the weather conditions were atrocious both in England, and Normandy and the German high command had let down its guard, convinced that the Allies would never land in such conditions. Rommel, in particular, had decided to head for Germany to celebrate his wife's birthday and to meet with Hitler.

However, the Allies had an advantage over their enemies. They had weather stations in the Atlantic, which enabled them to forecast an imminent improvement. And indeed, Group Captain Stagg, chief meteorological officer for the SHAEF, forecast a 36-hour improvement as from the 6th of June. Hence, after postponing the operation 24 hour, General Eisenhower finally gave the order to launch operation Neptune.

General Gale, chief of the 6th Airborne Division, haranguing his paras immediately prior to D-Day. © IWM

Bob de La Tour, Don Wells, John Vischer and Bob Midwood, the lieutenants from the 6th Airborne Division's four Pathfinder sections, synchronising their watches before heading for their aircraft. © IWM

At the Harwell aerodrome, these Pathfinders are blackening their faces before boarding the Albemarle that is waiting behind them. © IWM

Again at the Harwell aerodrome, night has fallen and the men are ready to board the Albemarle that will take them to Normandy. © IWM

Then came the final brief for the 6th Airborne unit before heading for the airfields from where they would take off. General Gale harangued his men one last time with a certain sense of prose, 'The Hun thinks only a bloody fool will go there. That's why I'm going.'

Five thousand parachutists harnessed themselves with incredible quantities of material then waited for long hours on the airstrip before boarding the 422 planes that would take them to their fate.

A stick of parachutists aboard an Albemarle. They are sitting on the floor in a position that is far less comfortable than aboard the Dakota, equipped with benches. © IWM

HAM AND JAM

Shortly before 11pm, six Halifax bombers, each one towing a Horsa glider, took off from the Tarrant Rushton base in Dorset. The 180 men from Major Howard's Ox and Bucks Company D squeezed into their wooden cabins. When the formation approached the coast above Cabourg just after midnight, the pilots released the tug plane cables and each glider continued

its route alone. However, visibility was poor and they relied essentially on their instruments (chronometers, compasses, speedometers and altimeters).

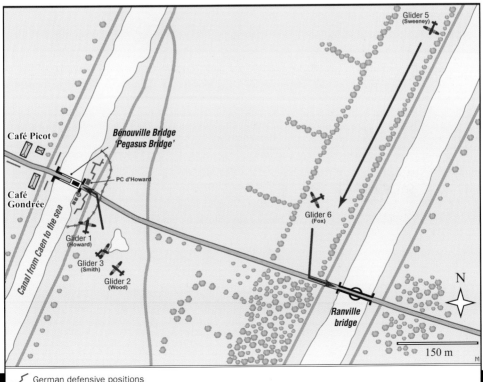

German defensive positions

After making almost a complete U-turn, Jim Wallwork and John Ainsworth, the pilots of Howard's plane finally located their target, Euston I, the bascule bridge at Bénouville. At 0.16am, Wallwork informed Howard that the landing was imminent and each man held onto his neighbour's arms and bent his knees. The overladen glider arrived too fast and hit the ground at over 95 mph. Ainsworth opened the parachute to slow down the craft. With its wheels torn off, the glider came to a halt amidst the German barbed wire defences around 45 yards from the bridge. A magnificent feat. However, the shock had been such that the two pilots had been ejected from the cockpit and were lying unconscious on the ground next to the glider. All the men in Howard's section had also passed out. The German guards at the bridge had heard the noise, but they thought that it had been caused by debris falling from a bomber, which happened quite frequently, and they paid no particular attention.

After ten seconds, which seemed like an eternity to Howard's men, they finally managed to squeeze their way out of the glider and they rushed to the bridge, led by Lieutenant Brotheridge. After having neutralised the bunker on the right bank, the airborne forces crossed the bridge at the double. Brotheridge then attacked a machine gun nest and was mortally wounded; however, his men finished the job and defeated the few defenders on the left bank. In the meantime, Lieutenant Wood's glider 2 had landed a minute after Howard's. Once more, the landing was so violent that Wood was ejected from the craft. As he regained his spirits, he joined Howard with his section and the latter ordered them to seize the trenches at the opposite side of the road, which they did so immediately.

Glider 91, in which Howard and Lieutenant Brotheridge's section crossed the Channel, a few yards from its target. © IWM

At this precise moment, glider 3 arrived. Barkway, the pilot, swerved to avoid hitting the first glider, but his fuselage split in two during the manoeuvre and the glider finally came to a halt on the edge of a pond, where Corporal Greenhalgh unfortunately drowned. Once more, under Lieutenant Smith's orders, the section regained consciousness and joined its fellow troops at the other side of the bridge. However, some men found themselves stuck inside the damaged fuselage.

Amidst the fighting, Captain Neilson's sappers discovered with relief that the bridge had not been booby trapped. Only the wires were in place and the explosive charges were found in a shelter nearby.

It was all over in just five minutes. At a cost of two dead, Bénouville bridge was now in Howard's hands and he eagerly awaited news from the other bridge in Ranville, around 400 yards away.

At 0.20am, Lieutenant Fox's glider 6 arrived 400 yards from its target, Euston II. As they approached the bridge, Fox's men were attacked by a machine gun that was finally neutralised by Sergeant Thornton's extremely accurate mortar fire. Fox was soon joined by Lieutenant Sweeney's section which had landed 700 yards to the north of the bridge. The last glider, commanded by Captain Priday, was nowhere to be seen. The pilot had mistaken the Dives for the Orne and had landed over 8 miles away. After a jaunt in a hostile environment, Priday's men finally joined their fellow paras on the night of the 6th to the 7th of June.

The Ranville bridge was under British control and two couriers were sent to inform Howard. He then ordered for the message 'Ham and Jam' to be sent to notify his superiors of the success of the operation. But, how would the Germans react?

What Howard dreaded most finally happened at 2am. The allied defenders could hear the sound of tracked vehicles. Tanks were heading towards the meagre airborne forces. But then, a sensational direct hit by

Aerial view of Euston II, the swing bridge in Ranville. We can clearly see Lieutenant Fox's section's glider. © IWM

The Ox and Bucks posing with a French girl sitting on a captured German motorcycle. Here, we can recognise the men from page 1, Captain Priday in the background, Corporal Lambley behind the young lady and Private Gardner with his Bren submachine gun to the right. © Pegasus Memorial Museum

Sergeant Thornton, armed with a PIAT antitank gun – not always a particularly efficient weapon – sent shells into the compartment of the leading tank, creating a huge explosion. Convinced they were facing heavily armed forces, the Germans withdrew. Meanwhile, Howard's long-awaited reinforcements were dropped in Dropping Zone N, to the north of Ranville. Brigadier Poett's 5th Brigade and the division's HQ, i.e. 2,000 men, jumped as from 0.50am. Although the zone was perfectly marked out, it was not always easy to located by night and, after two hours, only 60% of the men had reached their targets. At 3am, Lieutenant Colonel Pine-Coffin's 7th Battalion headed towards Bénouville to reinforce Howard's

John Howard

John Howard was 31 when he successfully accomplished the feat of capturing Bénouville bridge. From a modest family, he lived in London's West End and enlisted in the army at the age of 18, in the King's Shropshire Light Infantry Regiment. In 1938, he had completed his military service and left the army to become a policeman in Oxford. A year later he married Joy Bromley, whom he had met three years previously. They had two children. At the start of the war, he joined his regiment where he was rapidly promoted. In 1942, his unit became an airborne one and Major Howard was in command of Company D. After capturing Bénouville bridge, Howard was wounded twice during the Battle of Normandy. On his return to England, he was seriously injured in a car accident in November 1944, which rendered him immobile up to the end of the war. Despite his handicap, he returned to Bénouville every year to celebrate the great feat of his OX and Bucks. He died in 1999 at the age of 86.

Another view of the Ox and Bucks group. In the foreground, Lieutenant Smith's section's glider was split in two on landing. © IWM

positions. Meanwhile, the two other battalions, Lt. Col. Johnson's 12th and Lt. Col. Luard's 13th, destroyed the 'Rommel's asparagus' set by the Germans on the planned landing zone for the gliders, before taking up defensive positions to the south of Ranville.

At 3.20am, 50 gliders landed in the plain (Landing Zone N) that had been cleared by the parachutists. They brought with them the

Corporals Burton and Barnett from the Military Police keeping watch over a crossroads near Ranville on 9th June 1944. © IWM

rest of the division's HQ and General Gale, 1,200 extra men and 17 antitank guns. Satisfied with encouraging preliminary reports, Gale set up his headquarters at the Château du Hom.

Pegasus Bridge

Installed in 1935, this lift bridge was the only passageway over the canal linking Caen with the sea, to the north of the Normandy capital. After Howard's men's great accomplishment, the Germans sent a Focke-Wulf 190 fighter plane, which successfully managed to drop a bomb directly on the bridge roadway. By pure chance, the bomb did not explode, but bounced and fell into the canal. The impact can still be seen on the bridge. Two light boats were also sent from Caen and from Ouistreham, but one of

Pegasus Bridge. © Rights reserved

them grounded and the other turned back.
The bridge was officially baptised Pegasus Bridge on the 26th of June 1944, in reference to the British parachute force's insignia, the winged horse Pegasus. When the canal was enlarged in 1993, it was finally replaced by a similar bridge. The original Pegasus Bridge can now be admired within the Pegasus Memorial Museum in Ranville.

OTWAY NEUTRALISES
THE MERVILLE BATTERY

In Dropping Zone V, to the west of Varaville, the battalion chiefs struggled severely to group together their dispersed troops. The Pathfinders had jumped on the right spot, but their marking equipment had been lost in the marshes. *Flak* fire and strong westerly winds had also dislocated the Dakota formations. Consequently, the men from the 9th Battalion, who had received orders to neutralise Merville artillery battery, jumped without landmarks. When Lieutenant Colonel Otway reached the meeting point, few men were there to greet him. The five gliders transporting the material had also failed to arrive, having crashed to the depths of the English Channel.

© *Bundesarchiv*

After a two-hour wait, Otway only had 150 of the planned 750 men at his disposal. Material was in keeping: one single Vickers machine gun, six Bangalore torpedoes (out of 60) – long tubes filled with explosives that can be joined together and slid under barbed wire networks to destroy them – no jeeps, no mortars and no mine detectors. He nevertheless decided to engage in his mission with the meagre forces at hand.

Soldiers from the Merville battery garrison. It was served by 80 gunners from the 1716th artillery regiment and was defended by 50 sappers. © *Bundesarchiv*

Lieutenant Colonel Terence Otway

Born in Cairo in 1914, he joined the Royal Military Academy Sandhurst at the age of 19. He served in the Indian Army and his first taste of combat was in Shanghai, bombarded by the Japanese army. He married Stella Whitehead just before World War II was declared.

He was appointed at the War Office in 1942, where he studied the different operations launched by the British Army. The following year, he took command of the 9th Parachute Battalion. Seriously wounded by a shell on the 8th of June, he never returned to the front. In October, he was decorated with the Distinguished Service Order for his action in Merville.

He resigned from the army in 1948 to continue his career in different positions in trade and the press. A bust in his memory was inaugurated in Merville in 1997 and, four years later, he received the National Order of the Legion of Honour. He died in 2006 at the age of 92.

Near the site, he came across the men from the Troubridge Party, a small unit sent on reconnaissance. Sergeant Major Miller informed him that the bombing on the battery by 100 Lancasters had been ineffective. The group had nevertheless succeeded in opening a breach in the barbed wiring and in marking out passageways amidst the minefields without detection material.

Otway therefore completely reviewed his plan of attack. Whilst Sergeant Knight's group created a diversion at the main entrance, Major Parry led the main attack. However, all of a sudden two gliders, which at this point no one was expecting to see, emerged. Of the three unaccounted for, one had been forced to land in England after a problem with its towing cable, the second had landed around 2 miles away, and the third and last had decided to target the anti-aircraft gun in the battery and crashed around 700 yards from the site. The complete garrison was now on the look-out.

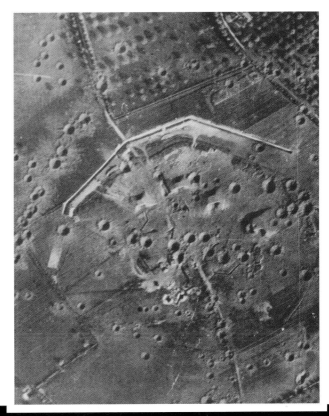

▲ On this aerial view dating from 1944, the antitank ditch can clearly be seen to the north and the ground is riddled with dolines caused by the bombardments that targeted the battery but failed to destroy its guns. © IWM

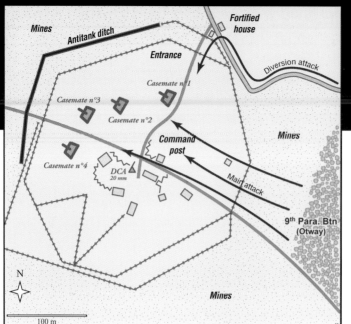

At 4.30am, the Bangalores exploded and the assault was launched. Covered on their left flank by the Vickers machine gun, the parachutists thrust across the minefield under deadly gunfire from the German defenders. Thanks to the gaps created by the Bangalores and even resorting to crawling across their fellow soldiers, laid down on the barbed wire, the Red Devils headed towards the four casemates. The trenches were the theatre of terrible hand-to-hand combat. The paras finally reached the *blockhaus* and launched grenades inside the air vents and through the openings. The garrison ended up surrendering. Otway was bitter. He had just lost half of his men to discover that the guns were of a lower calibre than expected. Parry's men successfully neutralised the artillery pieces with what they had at hand.

Otway then faced an urgent problem. Several men on the site were wounded and, without further news from him, *HMS Arethusa*, cruising off shore, was to fire on the battery to try to destroy it. However, neither the men nor the equipment to contact the battleship had reached Otway. A carrier pigeon was sent along with a yellow rocket that was thankfully seen aboard the *Arethusa*.

Fearing bombardment, the men left the site as quickly as they could and, with a severely weakened battalion, Otway withdrew to the village of Le Plein.

DESTRUCTION OF THE BRIDGES OVER THE RIVER DIVES

The drop on Dropping Zone K, to the west of Touffréville, was equally scattered as the one on DZ V. A share of the pathfinders had jumped near Ranville and had placed the beacons in the wrong zone. Consequently, two thirds of Pearson' 8th Battalion found themselves in DZ N. Two and a half hours later, only 120 men had joined their chief. Pearson split his group in two in order to accomplish his mission, the destruction of the Bures and Troarn bridges. In Bures, the parachutists joined forces with Captain Jukes' sappers and by 9.15am, both the rail and the road bridges had collapsed into the River Dives.

In Troarn, a group of sappers commanded by Major Rose-veare reached the outskirts of the village around 4am. But, to reach the bridge, they needed to cross the village. Roseveare and eight of his men jumped into a jeep with a trailer. After ma-king its way past the first barrage, the vehicle headed down the main street at full speed under enemy gunfire. No parachutist was killed, only one of them falling from the vehicle during the ride. The men then placed demo-lition charges in the bridge and created a 15-feet breach before setting off again. Later in the day, Captain Jukes finished the job Roseveare had started.

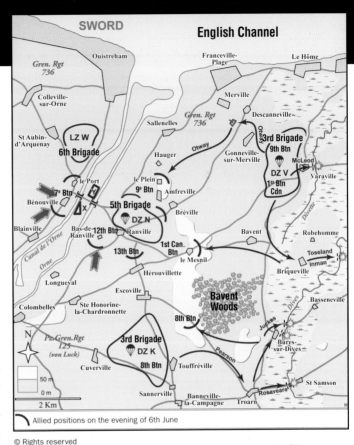

SWORD

English Channel

Gren. Rgt 736

Ouistreham

Franceville-Plage

Le Hôme

Colleville-sur-Orne

Merville

Sallenelles

Gren. Rgt 736

Descanneville

St Aubin-d'Arquenay

LZ W
6th Brigade

Hauger

Otway

Gonneville-sur-Merville

3rd Brigade
9th Btn

McLeod

le Port

le Plein

DZ V
1st Btn
Cdn

Varaville

7e Btn

9e Btn

Amfreville

Bénouville

5th Brigade

Bréville

Blainville

DZ N

Bas-de-Ranville

12th Btn

Ranville

Bavent

Robehomme

Canal de l'Orne

13th Btn

1st Can. Btn

le Mesnil

Toseland

Inman

Orne

Hérouvillette

Briqueville

Longueval

Escoville

Bavent Woods

Basseneville

Colombelles

Ste Honorine-la-Chardonnette

8th Btn

Jukes

Pz.Gren.Rgt 125 (von Luck)

3rd Brigade
DZ K

Bures-sur-Dives

Cuverville

8th Btn

Touffréville

Pearson

St Samson

Sannerville

Banneville-la-Campagne

Troarn

Roseveare!

N

50 m
0 m
2 Km

Allied positions on the evening of 6th June

This jeep with trailer belonging to the 716th RASC Company is quite representative of what Major Roseveare's team must have been like when it made its epic crossing through the village of Troarn. © IWM

Further north, the Canadians from the 1st Battalion met with the same misfortune as their British counterparts. A quarter of their total forces had reached target. Major McLeod took command of a group which spent the rest of the night defying the defenders of the Château de Varaville. McLeod was killed during the battle, but his unit managed to reach the bridge and destroy it before 8.30am.

South of Varaville, the few remaining men from Company B grouped together under the orders of Lieutenant Toseland. At 3am, the bridge at Robehomme was reached and 30 pounds of explosives only managed to shake the structure. Three hours later, Lieutenant Inman's unit completed the job.

▲ Canadian parachutists from Bradbrooke's 1st Battalion at rest in a transit camp shortly before D-Day.
© Library and Archives Canada

Bill Millin, Lord Lovat's piper, landing on Sword Beach with his British commando unit. Near his face, we can see the drone of his bagpipes. © IWM

These commandos from the 1st Special Service Brigade, wearing their green berets, have joined parachutists from the 6th Airborne in the streets of Bénouville. © IWM

ORDERS AND COUNTER ORDERS FOR THE *21. PANZER*

When Major von Luck, chief of the *Panzer Grenadier Regiment 125* was informed of the first parachute drops, he tried to contact his superior, General Feuchtinger, without success. Long hours were lost as he waited for the order to attack. Only units in direct contact with the parachutists launched attacks. Such was the case of the heavily armed *Panzer Grenadier Regiment 192* in Bénouville, before it was finally driven back by Pine-Coffin and Howard's men. Early the next morning, Von Luck ended up sending his 3rd Battalion to attack the British positions to the south of Ranville, with support

This group of parachutists from the 12th Battalion has just spent four days behind the enemy lines after having been dropped far from their Dropping Zone. After such misadventure, a good meal is always welcome. © IWM

from tanks. Fighting continued till midday, however, the Germans were driven back, in particular thanks to the antitank guns that had been positioned over the night.

These initial counter-attacks failed to prevent the junction between the troops landed on Sword Beach and Gale's paras. At 1pm, the parachutists entrenched around Bénouville bridge could hear the bagpipes played by Bill Millin, piper for Lord Lovat, commander of the 1st Special Service Brigade. The commandos from Sword came to reinforce the airborne troops over the night.

Meanwhile, the *21. Panzer* had finally received orders to counter-attack to the east of the Orne and, at 8am, began to head towards the paras, only to receive the counter order an hour and a half later to head in direction of the British troops landed on Sword Beach to the west of the river. Several more hours were wasted crossing the ruined city of Caen before being able to head north of the Norman capital. Two *Kampfgruppen* were formed, one of which managed to stop the British progression, whilst the other successfully reached the shoreline at Luc-sur-Mer, from where it could finally perceive the immense Allied armada out at sea.

After fierce combat to take control of the Riva-Bella casino, the French commandos fraternised with their compatriots. © IWM

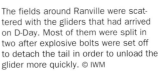

The fields around Ranville were scattered with the gliders that had arrived on D-Day. Most of them were split in two after explosive bolts were set off to detach the tail in order to unload the glider more quickly. © IWM

However, at 9pm, the planes and 248 gliders engaged in operation Mallard and transporting the 6th Airlanding Brigade, the last unit from the 6th Airborne Division, flew above them: 142 gliders headed for Landing Zone N in Ranville and the others for LZ W near Saint-Aubin-d'Arquenay. Fearing becoming isolated from the rest of their division, the *Panzergrenadiers* retreated back to Caen. The only *Panzerdivision* present on D-Day was finally incapable of sending the Allies back into the sea. Only Caen, which should by then have liberated, was still in German hands.

Hence, on the evening of the 6th of June, all the missions assigned to the 6th Airborne Division had been successfully accomplished: some 10,000 men were in action between the Orne and the Dives, but many had not yet joined their units. For the parachutists, then began three months of a long and exhausting war of positions to the east of the Orne. At last, on the 16th of August 1944, operation Paddle was to enable them to reach the opposite bank of the Dives and to head towards the Seine. The unit was finally withdrawn from the front as from September and repatriated to Great Britain. It had lost around 4,500 men (killed, wounded or unaccounted for).

A heavily laden glider could land at over 80mph and very quickly become impossible for the pilot to control. This is most likely what happened to this glider which ended up crashing into a house. © IWM

Today, there are several commemorative sites within the sector where the 6th Airborne Division was dropped. Steles mark the spots where Howard and his men, and Otway's 9th Battalion fought. A museum has been opened on the site of the Merville battery to tell the tale of the battalion's great feat. A magnificent C-47 Dakota stands before the entrance.

A few miles to the south, over 2,000 soldiers are laid to rest in the British cemetery in Ranville. And near to the church, the belfry of which was a precious landmark for many paras on the night of the 5th to the 6th of June, a stele has been installed in memory of Lieutenant Brotheridge, undoubtedly among the first allied soldiers to lose his life during the Landings.

But the most emblematic site of all is unquestionably the Pegasus Memorial Museum in Ranville. An earlier museum was inaugurated by General Gale in 1974, on the very site where Major Howard's men fought. This museum, built by the *Comité du Débarquement* (D-Day commemoration committee), presided over at the time by Raymond Triboulet, the first Sub-Prefect of Bayeux after the liberation, reunited a collection of objects recovered on the battlefield or donated by veterans, including Lord Lovat's piper Bill Millin's bagpipes. However, the museum was to close in 1997.

Private Emile Corteil and his dog Glen

Emile Corteil was enlisted in Lieutenant Colonel Otway's 9th Battalion. He was a dog handler and had been dropped along with his faithful four-legged companion, Glen. Just like many of his fellow paras from the 9th Battalion, Corteil and Glen landed in the wrong place. They waded their way through the marshes before joining a group of 38 paras commanded by Brigadier Hill, chief of the 3rd Brigade. Suddenly, allied bomber planes took the parachutists for Germans. Most of them were killed or wounded by friendly fire. Even Hill himself was seriously injured. Corteil and Glen were among the dead. They are buried together in the Ranville cemetery.

Private Emile Corteil and his dog Glen. © Rights reserved